# Emergency Trucks

Julie Murray

Abdo Kids Junior
is an Imprint of Abdo Kids
abdobooks.com

Abdo
TRUCKS AT WORK
Kids

**abdobooks.com**

Published by Abdo Kids, a division of ABDO, P.O. Box 398166, Minneapolis, Minnesota 55439.
Copyright © 2024 by Abdo Consulting Group, Inc. International copyrights reserved in all countries.
No part of this book may be reproduced in any form without written permission from the publisher.
Abdo Kids Junior™ is a trademark and logo of Abdo Kids.

Printed in the United States of America, North Mankato, Minnesota.

052023

092023

Photo Credits: Getty Images, Shutterstock, ©Washington State DOT p.22/ CC BY-NC-ND 2.0, ©Dawn Endico p.22/ CC BY-SA 2.0

Production Contributors: Teddy Borth, Jennie Forsberg, Grace Hansen

Design Contributors: Candice Keimig, Pakou Moua

Library of Congress Control Number: 2022946713

Publisher's Cataloging-in-Publication Data

Names: Murray, Julie, author.

Title: Emergency trucks / by Julie Murray

Description: Minneapolis, Minnesota : Abdo Kids, 2024 | Series: Trucks at work | Includes online resources and index.

Identifiers: ISBN 9781098266134 (lib. bdg.) | ISBN 9781098266837 (ebook) | ISBN 9781098267186 (Read-to-me ebook)

Subjects: LCSH: Trucks--Juvenile literature. | Vehicles--Juvenile literature. | Emergency vehicles--Juvenile literature.

Classification: DDC 388.32--dc23

# Table of Contents

Emergency Trucks....4

More
Emergency Trucks...22

Glossary............23

Index..............24

Abdo Kids Code.....24

# Emergency Trucks

Mary sees flashing lights.

It is an emergency truck!

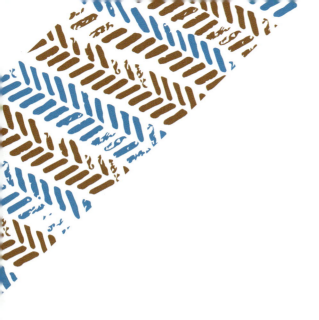

A house is on fire. A fire truck is there to help.

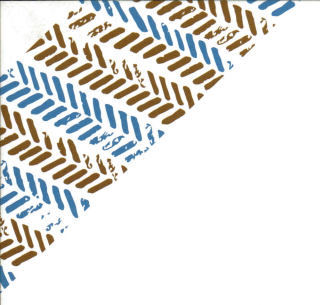

The ambulance truck moves hurt people to a hospital.

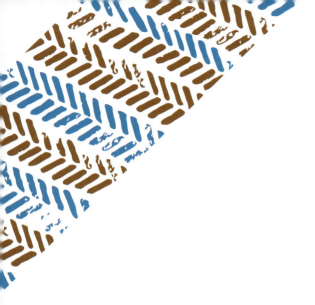

Ed's car broke down.

He called a tow truck.

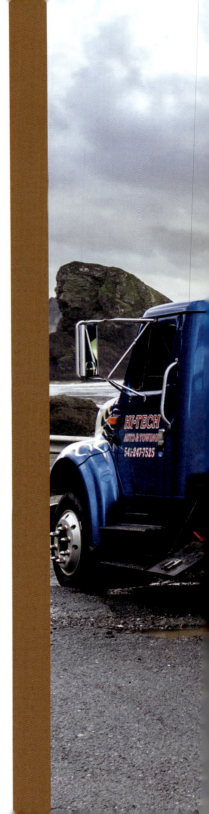

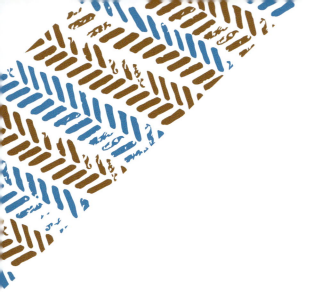

Eva drives a police truck.

She keeps people safe.

A water tender brings water to a fire.

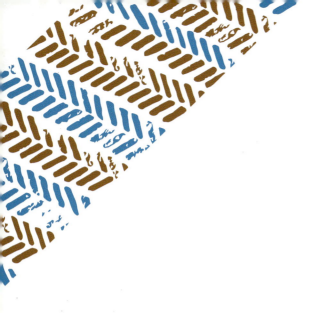

There was a bad accident.

A **heavy rescue** truck helps.

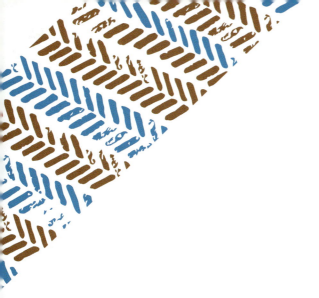

A **SWAT** truck is armored. It helps in unsafe situations.

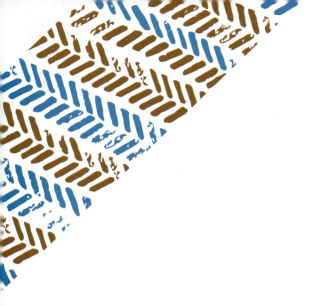

What emergency trucks have you seen?

# More Emergency Trucks

air supply truck

hazardous material truck

ladder truck

roadside assistance truck

# Glossary

**heavy rescue**
a response vehicle with tools and equipment to support rescue operations.

**SWAT**
short for Special Weapons and Tactics.

# Index

ambulance 8

fire truck 6

heavy rescue truck 16

police truck 12

SWAT truck 18

tow truck 10

water tender 14

Visit **abdokids.com** to access crafts, games, videos, and more!

Use Abdo Kids code **TEK6134** or scan this QR code!